Sizewell nuclear power station

U.S. SBN: 0-531-04183-2
Library of Congress
Catalog card No:
80-54727

*Published in the United
States*
1981 by
Franklin Watts
730 Fifth Avenue
New York,
New York 10019

Printed in Belgium

NUCLEAR

NIGEL HAWKES

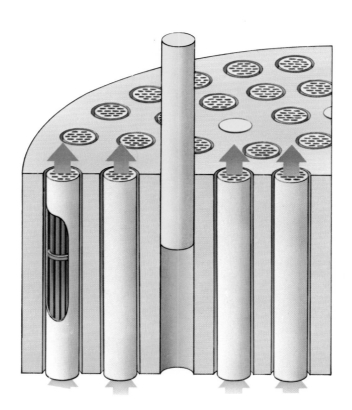

FRANKLIN WATTS
London · Toronto · New York · Sydney

Ray Dafter *is Energy Editor of the Financial Times. In 1978 he spent a year doing research at Harvard University, and lecturing in the United States. He has written two books on Energy, broadcasts on radio and television, and contributes to a number of publications.*

Until recently mankind had taken energy for granted. It was always there – why bother about what it is or where it comes from? But today people are worried. Suddenly we discover that we have been using up important stores of energy – oil, natural gas and coal – far too quickly. We must all of us think very seriously: where will our energy come from in the future? For there is nothing in the world that is not affected by energy – or the lack of it – as this book and others in the series will show.

Here we look at a form of energy developed by some of the greatest minds of the twentieth century – and the one that has aroused the greatest controversy – NUCLEAR. Besides its destructive capacity nuclear energy is important because it can be used to generate electricity. At a time when there is growing concern over our supplies of coal, oil and gas it makes sense to exploit this, our most powerful energy source. But the nuclear industry world-wide has met with considerable opposition on safety grounds, from those worried about hazards. It will be some time before its critics are satisfied – if ever.

RAY DAFTER: *Consultant Editor*

These are the world's energy sources. These can all be reached; some easily, others with rather more difficulty. The sun plays the principal role in this energy scheme. However, we do not at present use solar power in any great quantities – only indirectly. The sun nurtured all the plants and animals, that now millions of years later, we burn as fossil fuels – coal, oil and gas. We also use uranium to fuel nuclear power plants. It is impossible to replace some energy sources – but the sun, moon, wind and water are constant. These are the energy sources that will still be with us to tap in the future.

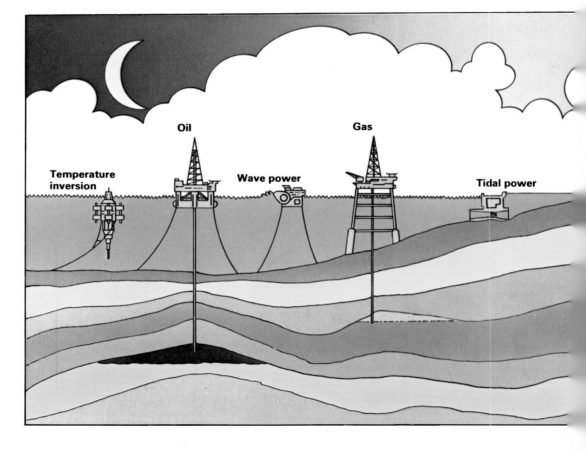

Contents

Art Director	Charles Matheson
Editor	Mike March
Art Editor	Ben White
Designer	David West
Typographic Design	Malcolm Smythe
Research	Dee Robinson
	Adam Martin
Illustrators	Denis Bishop
	Moira Chesmur
	Gary Hincks
	Peter Hutton
	Industrial Art Studio
	Jim Robins

Special thanks to the United Kingdom
Atomic Energy Authority for their
co-operation in the production of this book.

For the purpose of this book:
A billion is one thousand million. A trillion is
one million million.

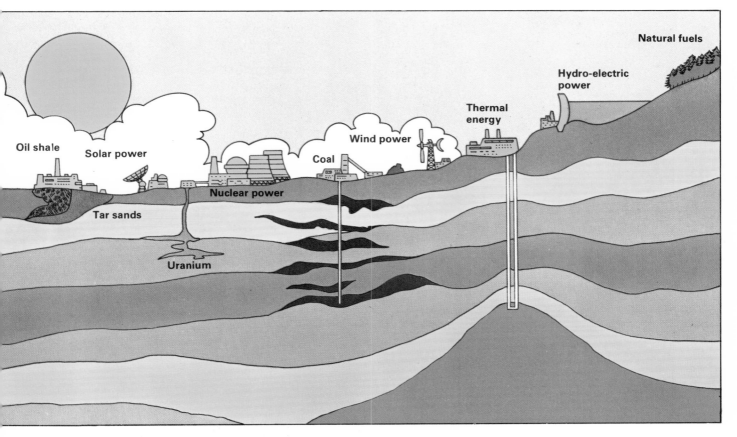

Nuclear power

Everything you can touch – every tree, every pebble, every drop of rain – consists of thousands of billions of atoms bound tightly together. The Sun, the stars, the Earth, the air, the oceans, are all assembled from atoms arranged in different ways. Atoms are too small to be seen, and for a long time they were thought to be the smallest particles into which matter could be divided. But in 1897, J. J. Thompson discovered an even smaller particle, the electron, a sub-division of the atom. It was only much later, however, that scientists discovered *how* to split the atom.

Nuclear power is the energy released when certain kinds of atoms are split. Inside a nuclear reactor this takes place in carefully controlled conditions. Nuclear weapons depend upon the same kind of atoms being split under very different conditions inside a bomb. In both cases, huge amounts of energy are released by the splitting of the atoms.

▷ All matter, from the burning fireball of the Sun to the tiniest twig, is made from atoms. Atoms are too small to see but they are the basic building blocks from which everything in the universe is assembled.

Oil rig

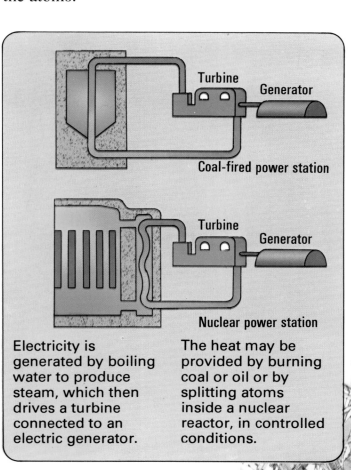

Turbine

Generator

Coal-fired power station

Turbine

Generator

Nuclear power station

Electricity is generated by boiling water to produce steam, which then drives a turbine connected to an electric generator.

The heat may be provided by burning coal or oil or by splitting atoms inside a nuclear reactor, in controlled conditions.

△ Most of our energy comes indirectly from the Sun. Fossil fuels – oil, coal and gas – are stores of energy from the Sun; winds, waves and waterpower are generated by its heat. But nuclear power is different.

In a nuclear reactor, the energy is used to boil water and produce steam, which in turn is used to drive steam turbines and generate electricity. In this respect there is no difference between a nuclear power station and a power station burning coal or oil; both use turbogenerators to convert their heat into electricity. Unlike coal or oil, however, nuclear power cannot be used for anything else but generating electricity. You cannot split atoms in a fireplace or use them to drive a car. This is because nuclear power needs complex engineering to control its release safely and thick shielding to prevent the escape of the dangerous products of atom splitting. Nuclear power stations are large and very expensive. They are designed to extract the awesome power of the atom in a safe and controlled way.

The first nuclear power stations were built in Britain and the United States in the 1950s. Today there are more than 200 nuclear power stations operating around the world, and many more under construction. Many believe that as resources of oil and coal decline, nuclear power will grow in importance. But nuclear power has its opponents, who argue that it is dangerous and unnecessary. They say it is a hazard to the environment and should be replaced by safer energy sources.

Strip coal mine

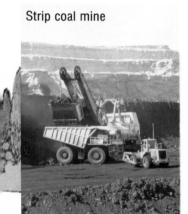

Gas rig

△ Supplies of coal, oil and gas must be constantly replenished to feed fuel to power stations. Extraction is often complicated, requiring advanced technology.

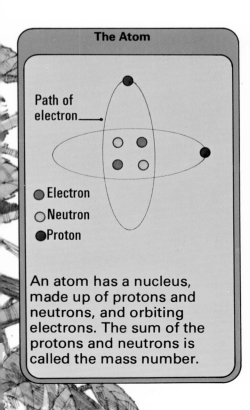

The Atom

Path of electron

- ● Electron
- ○ Neutron
- ● Proton

An atom has a nucleus, made up of protons and neutrons, and orbiting electrons. The sum of the protons and neutrons is called the mass number.

The Uranium Atom

Nucleus

Paths of electrons

The heavier the element, the bigger the atoms. Uranium is the heaviest naturally occurring element and has many protons and electrons.

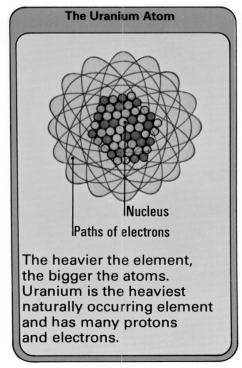

Isotopes of Uranium

Uranium-235 Uranium-238

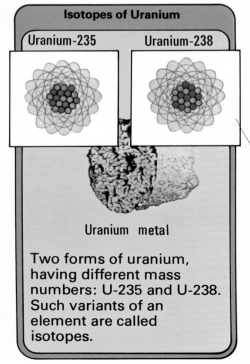

Uranium metal

Two forms of uranium, having different mass numbers: U-235 and U-238. Such variants of an element are called isotopes.

Splitting the atom

Fossil Fuel

When coal or oil is burned, heat is produced by the *chemical* reaction of combustion. The atoms are not changed, only rearranged.

Nuclear Fuel

When an atom of uranium splits, the energy comes from a *nuclear* reaction. The atoms are changed; a single heavy atom yields many lighter atoms.

Most atoms are very reluctant to be split. The nucleus at the center of the atom is held together by strong forces, and breaking these needs a lot of energy. That is why Lord Rutherford, one of the greatest of atomic physicists, doubted that the splitting of atoms would ever provide a source of power.

But Rutherford died in 1937, two years before an event which would have changed his mind. Otto Hahn and Lise Meitner, working in Berlin, discovered that atoms of the metal uranium would split quite easily. A single atom of uranium would divide into two lighter atoms in a process called fission. It was the most fateful discovery of the twentieth century.

Two things made fission of vital economic and military importance. The first was that it produced energy, but – equally importantly – once the process had begun, the uranium continued fissioning.

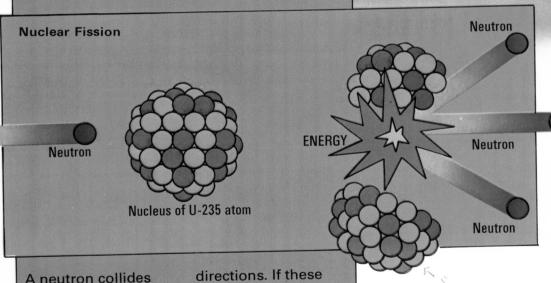

Nuclear Fission

Neutron

Nucleus of U-235 atom

ENERGY

Neutron

Neutron

Neutron

▷ The uncontrolled fission action of an atomic bomb needs uranium of the right type and a neutron to trigger it off.

A neutron collides with the unstable nucleus of the uranium atom, causing it to split. In splitting, the nucleus produces large amounts of energy and several new neutrons, which fly off in all directions. If these neutrons collide with more uranium nuclei, they will make them split too, producing still more neutrons. Given enough uranium, the process will accelerate uncontrollably.

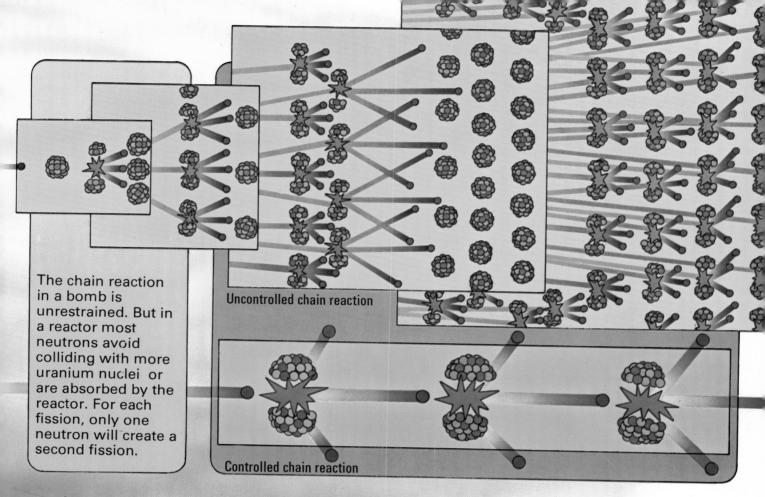

The chain reaction in a bomb is unrestrained. But in a reactor most neutrons avoid colliding with more uranium nuclei or are absorbed by the reactor. For each fission, only one neutron will create a second fission.

Uncontrolled chain reaction

Controlled chain reaction

△ In a nuclear power station, fission is controlled, producing a steady supply of heat to generate electricity from steam.

Every time a uranium nucleus was split by bombarding it with a particle called a neutron, it released energy – far more energy than was needed to produce the neutron required to split it. A single neutron was enough to make a uranium nucleus fission; but the process of fission itself produced several neutrons, which could go on and make other nuclei divide, producing yet more neutrons. So long as there were uranium atoms present, the process would continue at accelerating speed. It was a chain reaction. It was self-sustaining.

Why does fission produce so much energy? When the uranium atom divides, it produces two lighter atoms; but the weight of these two lighter atoms, added together, is less than that of the uranium atom which produced them. In the process of fission, the mass that seems to have disappeared has, in fact, been converted directly into energy. As Albert Einstein had found out, a little bit of mass converts into a great deal of energy. Hahn and Meitner had discovered in fission the most powerful and concentrated source of energy known to man.

Reactor fuel

Uranium, the fuel for the world's nuclear power, is a grayish metal first extracted from its ore in 1841. Until the discovery of fission it had no economic importance, but today is one of the most vital natural resources of all. It occurs naturally in minerals such as pitchblende and uranite, and as a minor part of many other minerals. Most of the world's supply of uranium comes from the USA, Canada, Australia, South Africa and Namibia, but other countries, including France, Gabon, Niger and India, have substantial reserves.

The ores are mined by underground techniques, or by strip-mining, taking special precautions to protect the miners from radiation. The metal is extracted from the ore by dissolving it in a mixture of acids and then extracting the metal from the solution. Total world reserves of uranium today stand at just around 2 million tons, with annual demand running at about 30,000 tons a year. As we already know, however, the uranium found in nature is not all of one kind; it is a mixture of different forms, known as isotopes.

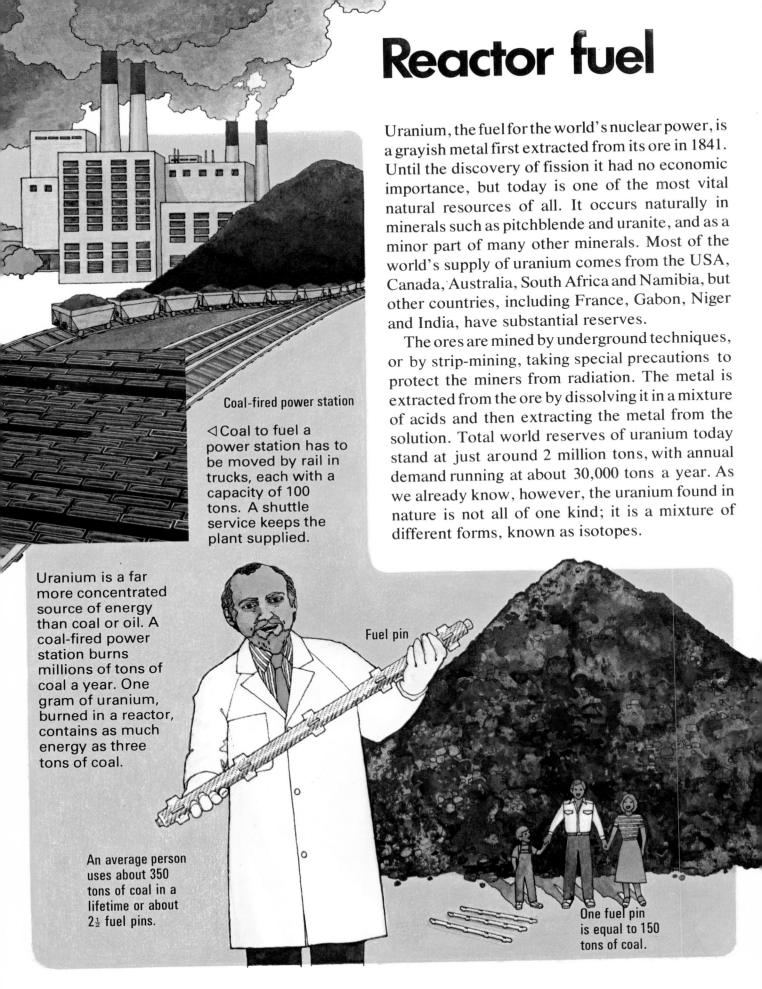

Coal-fired power station

◁ Coal to fuel a power station has to be moved by rail in trucks, each with a capacity of 100 tons. A shuttle service keeps the plant supplied.

Uranium is a far more concentrated source of energy than coal or oil. A coal-fired power station burns millions of tons of coal a year. One gram of uranium, burned in a reactor, contains as much energy as three tons of coal.

An average person uses about 350 tons of coal in a lifetime or about 2½ fuel pins.

Fuel pin

One fuel pin is equal to 150 tons of coal.

▷ Uranium may be mined by conventional deep mining techniques or (as here) by strip-mining. The layer of soil lying over the ore is removed with huge scrapers, exposing the ore, which can then be quarried out and taken away. The ore is then converted to uranium oxide.

The uranium fuel is enriched by separating the cream – uranium 235 – from the milk – uranium-238. Uranium oxide is converted into a gas, and passed through a succession of filters (top) or whirled around in a centrifuge (bottom).

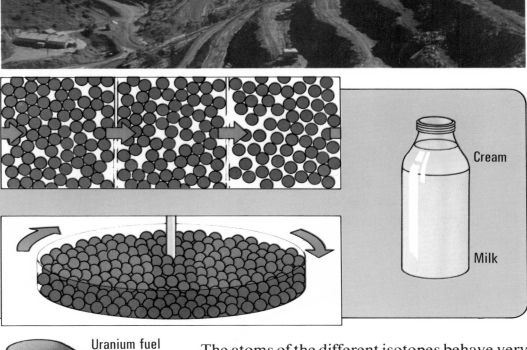

Cream

Milk

▽ Nuclear fuel consists of pellets of uranium dioxide, made by solidifying powdered oxide. They are packed into fuel pins which are then grouped for loading.

Uranium fuel

The atoms of the different isotopes behave very differently, and only one uranium isotope, uranium-235 (U-235), undergoes nuclear fission. In natural uranium, U-235 comprises less than 1 per cent of the total. The rest is almost entirely made up of the slightly heavier isotope uranium-238 (U-238).

Nuclear reactors can run on natural uranium, but normally the amount of U-235 in the fuel is increased artificially by the process known as enrichment. For most reactors, the U-235 is increased from the less than 1 per cent which occurs in nature to about 3 per cent.

The first reactors built used uranium metal as the fuel, but today uranium dioxide is more common. The dioxide in the form of powder is pressed to form solid pellets, which are then loaded into narrow tubes up to 3.7 m (12 ft) long, known as pins. The pins are mounted together side-by-side to form fuel elements, containing up to 200 pins, ready for feeding into the reactor.

How it works

All that is needed for fission to take place is a sufficient amount of U-235 and a source of neutrons to start it off. A simple nuclear weapon consists of little more than this. But a nuclear power plant, where a controlled release of energy is needed, is a much more complicated arrangement. There are certain basic principles that apply in the case of all reactors – whether gas-cooled, which is the commonest type in Britain, or water reactors, the type favored in the United States.

First, the reactor must run safely and steadily. This is achieved by controlling the flow of neutrons. The neutrons produced by fission are traveling at very great speeds, and in most reactors are deliberately slowed down by a material known as a moderator. Slow neutrons are much more likely, when they collide with the atoms of U-235, to cause a fission and keep the reaction going. A moderator is composed of light atoms, and the materials most commonly used are carbon (in the form of graphite) and water.

△ Fuel elements are loaded into the reactor at the top, using a mobile machine to insert fresh ones or remove ones used up.

Gas-cooled reactor

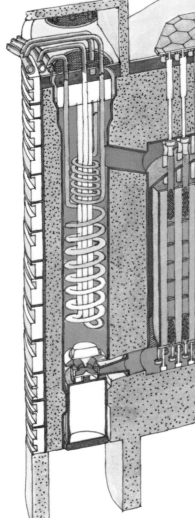

Reactor Core

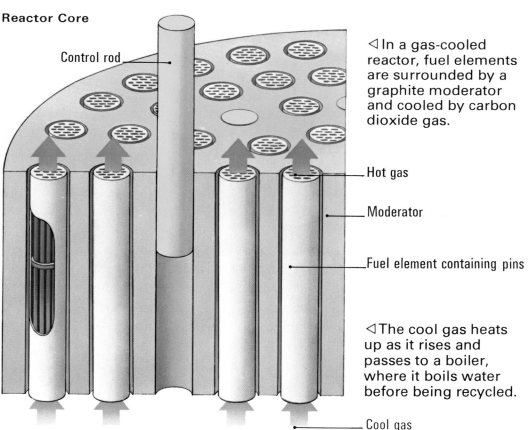

Control rod

Hot gas

Moderator

Fuel element containing pins

Cool gas

◁ In a gas-cooled reactor, fuel elements are surrounded by a graphite moderator and cooled by carbon dioxide gas.

◁ The cool gas heats up as it rises and passes to a boiler, where it boils water before being recycled.

The light atoms of the moderator collide with the neutrons, reducing their speed until they are moving no faster than the random to-and-fro movements of the atoms of uranium in the fuel. These random movements are caused by heat, and a neutron moving at the same speed as the atoms is called a thermal neutron. Similarly, the reactor is a thermal reactor.

For more precise control, rods of a neutron-absorbing material – called control rods – can be inserted into the core of the reactor. Pushed in, they soak up neutrons and slow down the reaction; pulled out, they allow it to speed up again.

The heat produced by the fission is removed by pumping gas or water past the hot fuel elements. Without a steady flow of coolant, the fuel would soon overheat and melt. The hot coolant is then passed through a heat exchanger and transfers its heat to water which boils, produces steam and generates electricity.

Because of intense radiation and the dangerous products of fission, the reactor is contained behind thick shielding, inside a huge vessel which can resist high pressures.

◀ Cold water in
▶ Hot steam out

◁ The reactor is mounted inside a pressure vessel (1). The reactor core (2) consists of many fuel elements held vertically, surrounded by a moderator (3) and with control rods (4) fitting between the fuel elements. Coolant gas enters at the bottom and leaves at the top, to flow downward again through the boilers (5) past coiled tubing which carries a flow of water. The hot gas heats the water to produce steam.

Shielding

Gas circulating pump

△ Steam from the reactor boilers passes into a large steam turbine, which turns an electricity generator mounted on the same shaft – as in a coal or oil-fired station.

The PWR

Originally developed to power nuclear submarines, the pressurized water reactor (PWR) has proven to be the world's most successful nuclear reactor. PWRs cost less to build than gas-cooled reactors and are cheaper overall, even though their fuel consumption is higher. The PWR uses enriched uranium dioxide fuel contained in pins made of an alloy of zirconium. It is both moderated and cooled by water, which flows past the fuel elements inside a thick-walled steel vessel at very high pressure.

▷ This PWR, generating 1,100 megawatts, has a pressure vessel (1) about 12 m (40 ft) high, 4 m (14 ft) in diameter and made of carbon steel 20 cm (8 in) thick. The vessel contains up to 200 fuel elements, each having some 200 fuel pins. The reactor is inside a building of steel-lined reinforced concrete, to contain radioactivity. Steam from the reactor goes to a turbine hall (2) to generate electricity, finally being condensed back to water again. The condenser is cooled by a water circuit and a cooling tower (3).

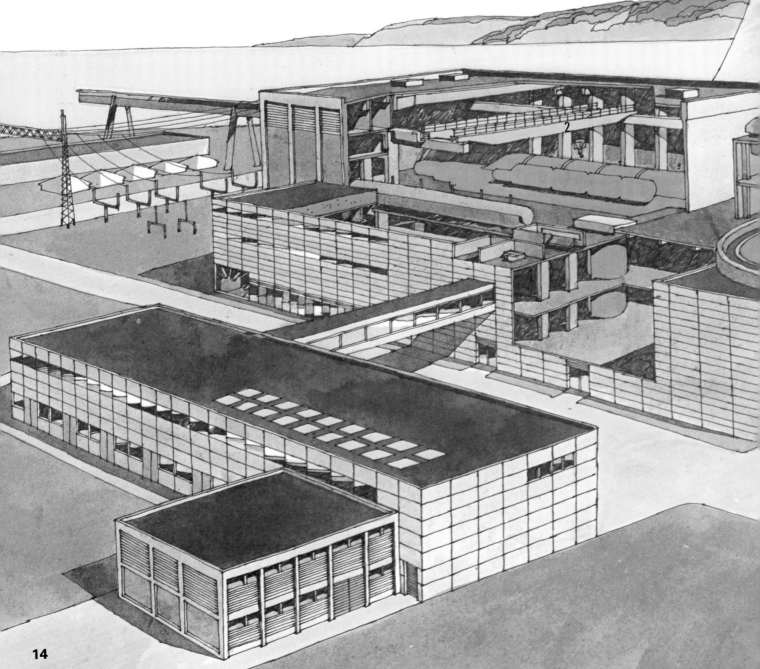

Because of the pressure, the water does not boil although its temperature is well above its normal boiling point. It passes, still under pressure, through a heat exchanger where it gives up its heat to a second water circuit, which is at normal pressure. The water in this second circuit boils, produces steam at about 300°C (600°F) and drives a steam turbine coupled to an electric generator.

The greatest danger with a PWR is an accident in which the supply of cooling water is interrupted or lost. The reactor is then immediately shut down ("scrammed") and the emergency core-cooling system comes into operation, flooding the core with cold water to prevent overheating.

All the fuel the reactor needs for about one year's operation is installed at the beginning. By the end of the year, not all the uranium has fissioned, but enough has been burned to slow the reactor down and ultimately stop it. Before this happens the spent fuel is removed and fresh fuel inserted. In a year's operation, a PWR generating 1,000 megawatts of electricity – enough to supply a large city – will use only about 1.5 tons of U-235.

There are other types of water-moderated reactors besides the PWR, just as there are different gas-cooled, or graphite-moderated reactors. Some of these use heavy water as a moderator – that is, water in which the hydrogen is replaced by deuterium, or heavy hydrogen.

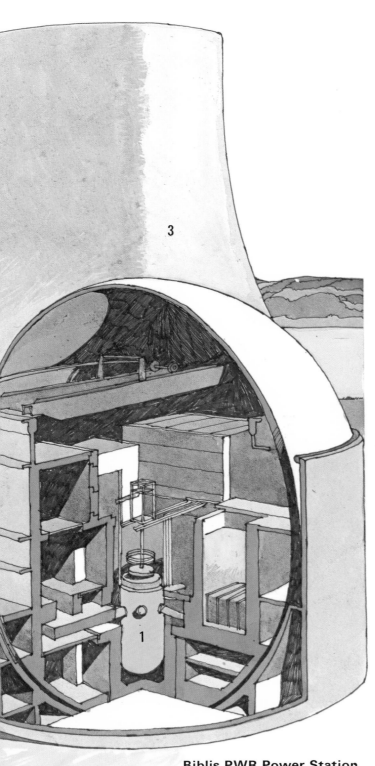

Biblis PWR Power Station

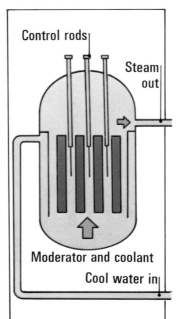

◁ A thick-walled steel pressure vessel contains the reactor, surrounded by water which acts as a coolant and moderator. The fuel is arranged as a series of vertical rods, and the water flows continuously past them. The water is heated to about 300°C (600°F) but does not boil because the pressure inside the steel vessel is 175 kg/cm² (2,500 lb/in²). The hot water is used to raise steam in an unpressurized circuit.

Control rods

Steam out

Moderator and coolant

Cool water in

Energy supply

Everybody wants electricity. It is the most versatile form of energy, able to provide lighting, heating and motive power efficiently and instantly. Today the cheapest way of generating electricity is with nuclear power, although at present this is by no means the major source of the world's, or indeed of any single country's, electricity supply. Nuclear power stations are more expensive to build than coal or oil-fired plants, but they consume less fuel, and their running costs are lower. Only hydro-electric plants offer a lower running cost, and their use is limited by the natural environment.

Because they are cheap to run, it makes sense to run a nuclear plant all the time, 24 hours a day, seven days a week. In practice, this is difficult to achieve because of unexpected breakdowns, and because at least once a year the plant must be shut down for routine maintenance and refueling.

▽ The electricity travels across the country through high voltage cables. All power stations are connected to the same distribution grid.

▷ The whole electricity grid is controlled from this room, the demand at any time determining how many power stations are used.

▷ Electricity is the most useful form of energy. It provides light and heat, and power for industry and the railways.

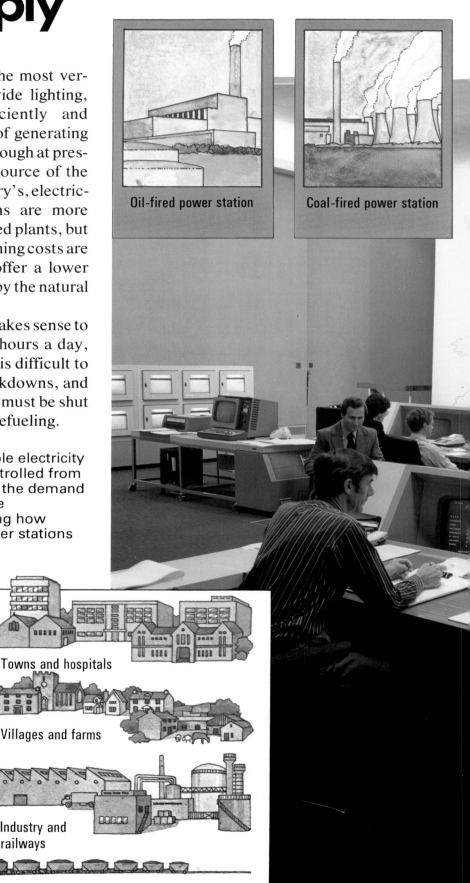

Oil-fired power station

Coal-fired power station

Towns and hospitals

Villages and farms

Industry and railways

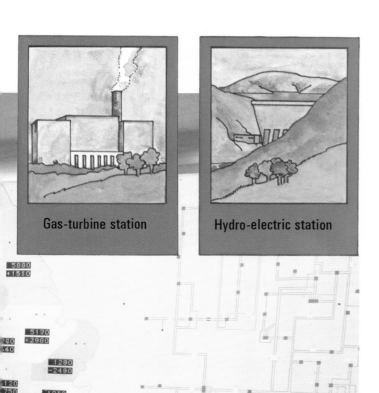

Gas-turbine station | Hydro-electric station

A typical nuclear plant probably runs for about 65–70 per cent of the time, averaged over the whole year. Some plants can be refueled without stopping them, which is an advantage. Others, including the PWR, cannot. They must be refueled during a period of the year when electricity demand is at its lowest, and this takes at least two weeks.

Demand for electricity varies during the year. The lowest demand in Europe occurs in the summer, but the opposite is true in many parts of the USA where air conditioning creates a bigger demand in summer than in winter. Demand also rises and falls during each day, the greatest demand occurring during the middle of the day, when heavy industrial loads coincide with a peak in domestic use.

Nuclear power plants cannot follow this varying pattern without lowering efficiency and so incurring additional costs. An electricity system also requires other types of plant for its energy supply. Sometimes coal and oil-fired plants are left with their turbines spinning and their boilers hot, ready to meet a sudden surge in demand. As demand falls, the controllers shut down power stations one after the other, starting with those with the highest running cost and finally, when demand is lowest at dead of night, leaving only a few nuclear and other low-cost plants still running.

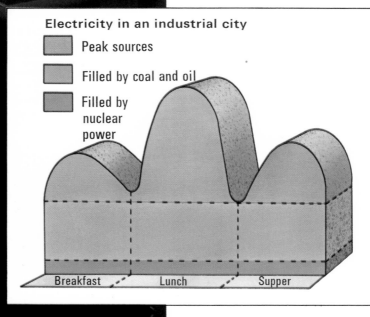

Electricity in an industrial city

☐ Peak sources
☐ Filled by coal and oil
☐ Filled by nuclear power

Breakfast · Lunch · Supper

Demand for electricity is not constant. As people's activities change, so does their need for electricity. There is a peak of demand at lunch time. Nuclear power is too inflexible to follow this varying pattern, so it only provides the base load. The peaks are filled by oil-fired or gas-turbine plants.

Working with atoms

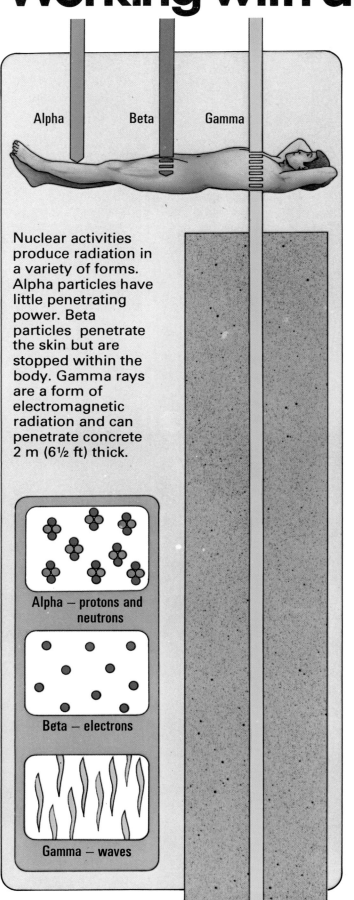

Alpha   Beta   Gamma

Nuclear activities produce radiation in a variety of forms. Alpha particles have little penetrating power. Beta particles penetrate the skin but are stopped within the body. Gamma rays are a form of electromagnetic radiation and can penetrate concrete 2 m (6½ ft) thick.

Alpha — protons and neutrons

Beta — electrons

Gamma — waves

Nuclear fission produces radiation as well as heat. Radiation is dangerous: it can kill or injure anybody exposed to enough of it. It can cause cancers to develop many years later, or even damage the body in such a way that children born later are affected by it. Those who work with atoms must be protected from all these dangers.

Radiation cannot be seen, heard, touched or smelled. But it can be detected by a variety of different instruments used in the nuclear industry. These will, among other things, show the radiation level, warn a worker if this is too high and record the duration of his exposure.

The first defense against radiation is to keep away from it; the greater the distance from the source, the lower the level of radiation. Once a reactor has begun operations, nobody will set foot again inside the reactor core, where the radiation levels are highest. All operations inside the reactor will be carried out by remote control, using very reliable machines designed to last the lifetime of the reactor without servicing.

▽ Many radioactive materials are handled remotely in concrete caves with thick lead-glass windows. Wherever such materials are being stored or transported you will see this warning sign.

Radiation symbol

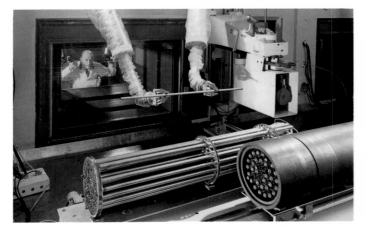

▽ Workers in contact with radioactivity wear protective clothing and carry devices which measure their exposure. This must never exceed a certain level.

▷ Anybody working in a nuclear plant must be checked regularly to see if they are contaminated. If so, careful washing and a decontamination check are called for.

Personal air sampler indicates exposure to airborne radioactive particles. _____

Film badge records whole body radiation exposure. _____

Quartz fiber electrometer registers radiation exposure at any given time. _____

Dosemeter gives an audible warning at a preset radiation level. _____

Coveralls _____

Emergency Clothing

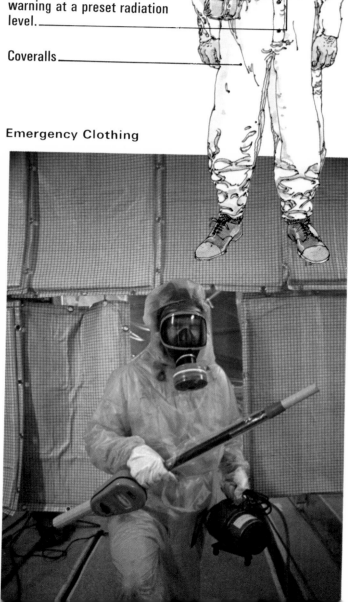

The second defense is shielding. Most forms of radiation cannot penetrate the thick concrete shield that surrounds the reactor, and fuel that has been inside the reactor is always removed by a heavily shielded fueling machine, transported in thick steel flasks and handled remotely behind thick panes of lead glass.

The third defense is time. The effects of radiation depend both on its intensity and the amount of time an individual is exposed to it. Every worker is continuously monitored by film badges or other radiation detectors, so that even if he is exposed it will be for such a brief time that he will suffer no ill effects.

These precautions are typical of the nuclear industry's concern for safety. Its spokesmen claim a far better track record for safety than is to be found in comparable industries. Radiation standards are set by the International Commission on Radiological Protection, and are accepted by all countries with nuclear facilities.

Pros and cons

△ In Europe and the USA, antinuclear protest has already delayed the building of many plants. The accident at Three Mile Island (right) did not help the nuclear cause. Although things could have been much worse, there were many demonstrations.

In 1973, the oil-producing countries of the Arab world, and others, imposed a sudden and steep increase in the price of oil, threatening supplies to the advanced countries. Oil was being used as a political weapon – a tap that could be turned on or off – and there seemed to be no limit to the price that might one day be charged for it. Alarmed by this prospect, the major oil-consuming nations have increasingly turned their attention to nuclear power as an alternative source of energy. It was thought to be dependable and it was available. Uranium deposits would last for a very long time, and fuel supply was not likely to be affected by politics or sudden price rises. At the same time, however, the growth of the nuclear industry has given rise to a powerful and articulate opposition movement.

The critics say that nuclear power stations are expensive to build, difficult to repair and often perform less efficiently than had been predicted. They stress the dangers of nuclear plants and the possible catastrophic consequences of an accident in which radiation is released.

Reactors Worldwide

Canada	United States	France	United Kingdom	Netherlands	Sweden	West Germany	USSR	Japan
10	69	14	33	2	6	12	25	20

Spain	Italy	Switzerland	Belgium
3	4	3	3

△ Most of the world's nuclear plants are found in the West and in Japan and the USSR. They were the first to develop nuclear power to meet their huge demands for electricity. Others are now copying them.

▷ After 25 years of development, nuclear power still represents only a small proportion of world-wide generating capacity and total energy use. But it is expected to grow more rapidly than other energy sources.

Nuclear Electricity Worldwide

7%

93% Electricity from other sources

Nuclear Electricity per Country

U S S R 30%	
Sweden 21.5%	
Belgium 21.3%	
France 15.8%	
United Kingdom 11.6%	
United States 11.5%	
West Germany 11.2%	
Japan 10.8%	
Canada 9.1%	
Netherlands 6.2%	
Spain 5.6%	
Italy 1.6%	

There are, they claim, examples of near disasters spanning over 20 years, from the fire at the Windscale plant, in England, in 1957, to the frightening events at Three Mile Island, Pennsylvania, where a reactor overheated through loss of coolant. Opponents also see the presence of nuclear power as a permanent threat to world peace. Why run all these risks, they ask, to produce a source of energy that is less versatile than fossil fuels and can only be used to generate electricity?

Supporters argue that the dangers are exaggerated. Despite what *might* have happened, they point out, there were no deaths at Three Mile Island. As to efficiency, they maintain that what has been said of nuclear plants is also true of plants burning coal and oil: some simply perform better than others.

It is vital, they believe, to replace oil by nuclear power whenever possible. With the world facing an energy crisis, they argue, this is no time to be giving up a technology which, despite its faults, can keep the lights burning and the wheels of industry turning well into the next century.

Nuclear engines

Why can't you drive a car by nuclear power? You could, but it would be a pretty odd sort of vehicle. The smallest reactor it is possible to imagine would need about 1 kg (2¼ lb) of pure U-235, which would cost tens of thousands of pounds to extract and enrich. Worse still, there would be the problem of shielding the passengers and passersby from radiation.

Even the simplest kind of shielding would be a sphere of at least 2.7 m (8 ft) across and weighing about 70 tons. And then there would be the danger of accidents, with catastrophic releases of radioactivity. Nuclear-powered cars just don't make sense. The same arguments apply even more strongly to the use of nuclear power in aircraft.

But nuclear propulsion is practicable in ships. Oil tankers and aircraft carriers are such huge vessels that nuclear reactors can be fitted into them quite easily. And in submarines nuclear propulsion offers the possibility of traveling at full speed, underwater, right round the world without refueling – an enormous military advantage over conventional submarines.

△ Nuclear submarines can stay underwater for months, traveling at full speed. Unlike other submarines, they do not have to surface at regular intervals to recharge their batteries.

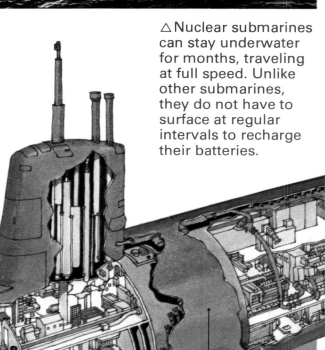

PWR reactor behind shield

Nuclear submarines are the most impressive demonstration of nuclear energy outside power stations. They use small pressurized water reactors, driving steam turbines.

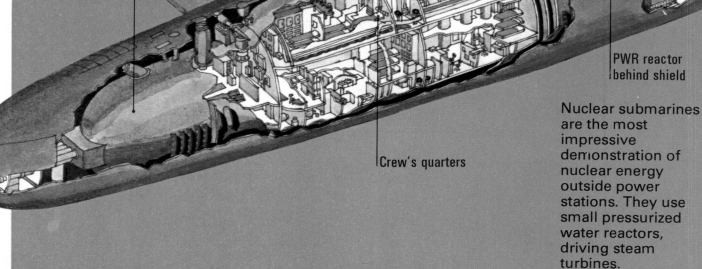

Nuclear-Powered Submarine

Warheads

Crew's quarters

△ Nuclear merchant ships can be unpopular. Here the Japanese vessel *Mutsu* is locked in by fishermen.

Turbine room

Nuclear submarines operated by the American and British navies use small PWRs to provide power and have operated successfully for many years. The U.S. Navy has also operated three nuclear-powered aircraft carriers, and the Soviet Union has built an ice-breaker, the *Lenin*, driven by a nuclear power plant.

Commercial nuclear ships have been less successful. They are expensive to build and operate, and most of those that have been built are no longer operating. If there were too many nuclear ships it would increase the risk of a collision at sea and the escape of radioactivity. At the moment, there seems to be little future for commercial nuclear ships, and the situation is only likely to change if the price of fuel oil gets much higher.

A nuclear-powered rocket has been designed by the U.S. National Aeronautics and Space Administration (NASA) and successfully tested on the ground, but has never flown in space. It uses a nuclear reactor to heat hydrogen to 2,200°C (4,000°F), discharging it through a nozzle to provide thrust. It could be used to take a manned vehicle to Mars, but fears about the dangers of launching a nuclear reactor into space have dissuaded the Americans from the idea.

▷ Both Canada and the USSR have designed nuclear-powered ice-breakers, which can operate in the northern oceans all winter long without having to refuel. Here the Soviet vessel *Lenin* cuts a path for a large cargo-carrier through the sea-ice.

Radioisotopes

As well as generating electricity, nuclear reactors can be used to produce exotic forms of matter which have many uses. We have already seen that uranium occurs naturally as a mixture of different forms, called isotopes. So do many other elements, but even those which have no naturally occurring isotopes can be changed into artificial isotopes by putting them inside a nuclear reactor and bombarding them with neutrons. The products of the bombardment are unstable, tending to revert to their natural form by giving off radiation in a process known as radioactive decay. Radioactive isotopes, whether naturally occurring – as in the case of U-235 – or, as in many other cases, produced artificially, are called radioisotopes.

For example, if the normal form of iodine, I-127, is bombarded with neutrons, it will form the radioactive isotope I-128. Chemically, it is identical with its parent, I-127, but its nucleus has absorbed a neutron, increasing the mass of the atom and producing a form not found in nature.

△ Radioisotopes can be used for medical diagnosis. Radiation from an isotope passes from a source through the patient to expose a film, rather like an X-ray. Radioisotopes are also used to sterilize medical equipment.

Half-Life Ratios

Each radioisotope has its own rate of decay, measured by the half-life. This is the time taken for the radioactivity to halve its value. The curve of the half-life graph will be the same for every radioisotope, irrespective of the time-scale involved.

Radioactivity

Time

I-128 gradually decays back to I-127, giving off beta radiation in the process. In any sample of I-128, half of it will have changed back to I-127 in 25 minutes; this time is called the half-life of the isotope. I-128 is not the only isotope of iodine which can be artificially produced by bombardment with neutrons inside a nuclear reactor. In fact, 21 iodine isotopes have been produced, with half-lives varying from as little as $2\frac{1}{2}$ seconds to as much as 1,720 million years (I-129). Altogether, about 1,400 isotopes of the hundred or so known elements have been produced.

Radioisotopes have many uses. They can be used as sources of radiation for medical treatments; cobalt-60, which gives off penetrating gamma rays, is used to treat cancer. The cobalt-60 is placed close to the cancerous tissues and the gamma rays destroy them. One of the most important uses of radioisotopes is as tracers – particularly in medical diagnosis. For example, the circulation of blood in the body can be studied by injecting a small amount of radioactive sodium-24 and then watching its movement around the body with a radiation detector.

△ Isotopes also have industrial uses, for discovering faults in vital components. Here a source is used to check the turbine blades in a jet engine. Radiation from the source penetrates the blades, passing through to expose the film arranged around the outside of the engine. Any hidden cracks show up as a result.

Reprocessing

A nuclear reactor stops operating long before all its U-235 has been consumed by fission. Products of fission collect inside the fuel elements, absorbing neutrons and slowing the reactor down. Before it stops completely, the fuel elements are taken out for the next step in the nuclear fuel cycle – reprocessing.

The purpose of reprocessing is to recover from the spent fuel the unused U-235 so that it can be recycled for use in a fresh fuel element. But it has another, and equally important, purpose. The neutrons flowing through the fuel have transformed some of the non-fissile isotope, U-238, into an altogether new element, plutonium. And one of the plutonium isotopes, Pu-239, is fissile, just like U-235. It can be used for nuclear weapons or for fueling nuclear reactors. So Pu-239, like U-235, is worth recovering from the spent fuel. But reprocessing is one of the most dangerous parts of the nuclear fuel cycle.

△ Spent fuel is removed from the reactor for reprocessing, using a fuelling machine. After a year of burning in the reactor, much of the uranium has been consumed, and new isotopes including plutonium are produced.

Fueling machine

▽ To allow some radioactivity to die away and make the spent fuel element easier to handle, it is kept for a few months in a storage pond.

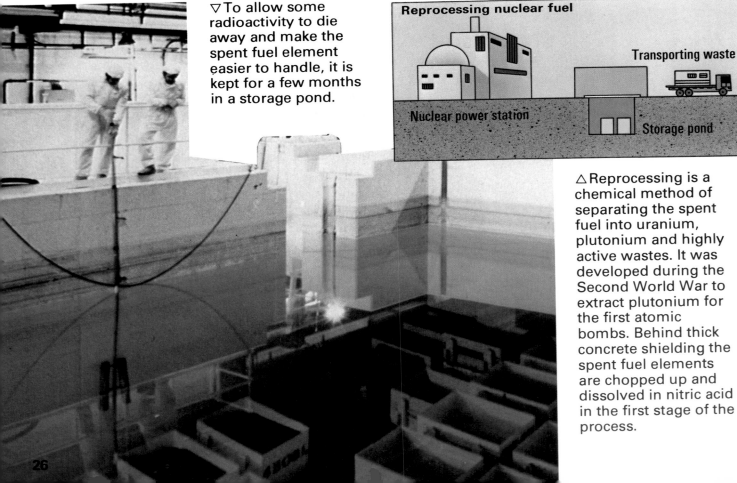

Reprocessing nuclear fuel

Transporting waste

Nuclear power station

Storage pond

△ Reprocessing is a chemical method of separating the spent fuel into uranium, plutonium and highly active wastes. It was developed during the Second World War to extract plutonium for the first atomic bombs. Behind thick concrete shielding the spent fuel elements are chopped up and dissolved in nitric acid in the first stage of the process.

◁ The spent fuel contained in 70-ton steel "flasks", is carried by road or rail from the power stations to reprocessing plants, such as Windscale, England (top). These flasks must be completely accident proof. They are tested by dropping them onto sharp steel spikes or by driving trains into them.

The recovery is done by a chemical process, under remote control and shielded behind concrete. The fuel elements are dissolved in nitric acid and chemically separated into three streams – one carrying uranium, one carrying plutonium, and the third carrying the poisonous and very radioactive wastes from the fission reaction.

The spent fuel when it comes out of the reactor is highly radioactive, and must be carried to the reprocessing plant in huge "flasks" made of steel 36 cm (14 in) thick. The plant itself is heavily contaminated and cannot be entered for repairs. It must therefore be in perfect working order and "fail safe".

The reprocessed uranium, which makes up about 98 per cent of the fission products, is returned to the fuel fabrication plant for making into new fuel elements. The small quantity of plutonium recovered, about 1 per cent, is for the moment stored but will also one day be used for fueling a reactor. The highly dangerous waste – the third stream – must be stored in complete security for several hundreds of years.

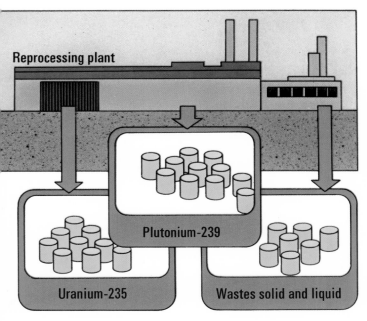

Reprocessing plant

Plutonium-239

Uranium-235

Wastes solid and liquid

△ The nitric acid solution is mixed with an organic solvent called Butex. The uranium and plutonium move into the solvent stream, leaving the fission products in the acid, and are separated in a second solvent extraction step. Thus the output of reprocessing is three streams: uranium, plutonium and waste.

Nuclear waste

One thing that distinguishes nuclear power from all other forms of energy is what is left behind after the fuel is burned – the "ash" of nuclear fission. In the reprocessing plant, uranium and plutonium are recovered, as we have seen, leaving a mixture of highly radioactive isotopes that cannot be used for anything, yet cannot be thrown away because they are so lethal.

Dealing with waste is one of the toughest problems the nuclear industry has to face. The quantities involved are not very large, but the waste contains radioisotopes that will take many hundreds of years to decay to a safe level. Throughout that period they must be prevented from escaping and contaminating air, water or soil. So far no foolproof method of achieving this has been found.

As the waste comes out of the reprocessing plant, in the form of a solution in nitric acid, it passes through stainless steel pipes into special tanks where it is stored. Because of the radioactive decay heat, the solution must be kept cool to prevent it from boiling away.

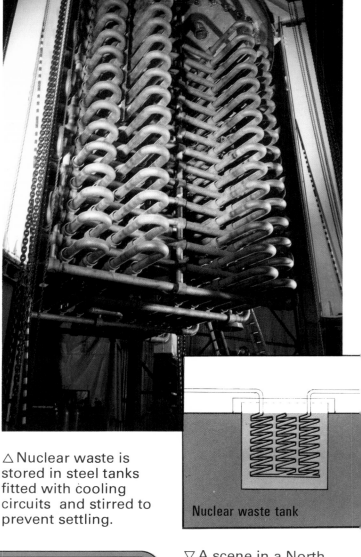

△ Nuclear waste is stored in steel tanks fitted with cooling circuits and stirred to prevent settling.

Nuclear waste tank

▷ Coal-fired plants use huge volumes of fuel and produce a lot of waste, most of it harmless. But sulphur dioxide, produced from traces of sulphur in the coal, has been blamed for making rain acid and killing fish. Mining coal is dirty and dangerous.

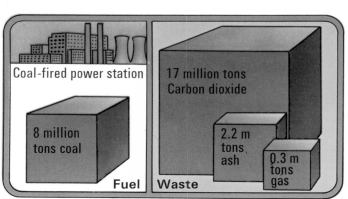

Coal-fired power station

8 million tons coal

Fuel

17 million tons Carbon dioxide

2.2 m tons ash

0.3 m tons gas

Waste

▷ Nuclear plants use very little fuel and produce little waste; but this is deadly and must be stored safely. Low active waste – used glassware, contaminated clothing, and so on – is less dangerous. Uranium and plutonium are stored or recycled.

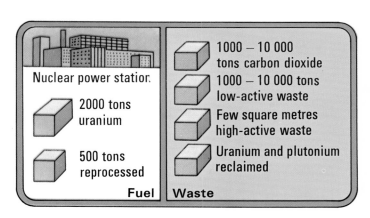

Nuclear power station

2000 tons uranium

500 tons reprocessed

Fuel

1000 – 10 000 tons carbon dioxide

1000 – 10 000 tons low-active waste

Few square metres high-active waste

Uranium and plutonium reclaimed

Waste

▽ A scene in a North American desert. Nuclear waste contained in drums is dumped by crane.

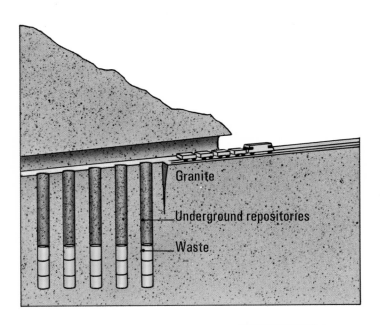

▷ In future, highly active waste may be turned into glass and left in underground repositories drilled into granite, salt or clay. The sites must be chosen so that no radioactivity can leak into underground water supplies.

▷ Low-active waste from German power stations is stored underground in a disused salt mine.

The storage tanks are themselves made of stainless steel and fitted with cooling circuits and agitators to prevent solids from settling at the bottom. The tanks at Windscale, in England, are surrounded by a second stainless steel jacket, inside a concrete shield, which is itself lined with stainless steel. The tanks do not provide a long-term solution to the storage of waste. Even stainless steel will begin to leak after about 50 years, although this is much better than mild steel. (Leaks in the ordinary mild steel storage tanks at the Hanford plant in the state of Washington, began to develop about 20 years after the waste was stored.)

Nuclear waste may be safer in the form of a solid. One way of achieving this is to mix the waste with the minerals used to make glass, and to heat the mixture in a kiln until it fuses together into a glassy solid. The molded pillars of glass might then be stored underground for long periods, without requiring constant attention. Other more far-fetched suggestions include firing the waste into the Sun on board a rocket, or simply leaving the waste on the ice shelf in the Antarctic and allowing its decay heat to melt a path down through the ice to the rocks below.

What might go wrong

After it has been running for a little while, a nuclear reactor will already contain very large quantities of radioactive material produced by the fission process. This material must at all costs be kept inside the reactor. If it were to be released – in the worst possible kind of accident – it could have devastating effects, perhaps killing and injuring hundreds of thousands of people.

In practice, not all the radioactivity can be contained. Very tiny amounts do escape into the air and water around the plant. But the amounts are so small that they are not thought to be a hazard. The radiation dose received by an average member of the public from nuclear plants is only one hundredth of what he gets from natural background radiation from soil and rocks, and about one fifteenth of that received from medical X-rays. Spokesmen for the industry claim that if you lived next door to a nuclear power station you would stand less chance of being killed by its operations than if you smoked just one cigarette a year. But what if something were to go badly wrong?

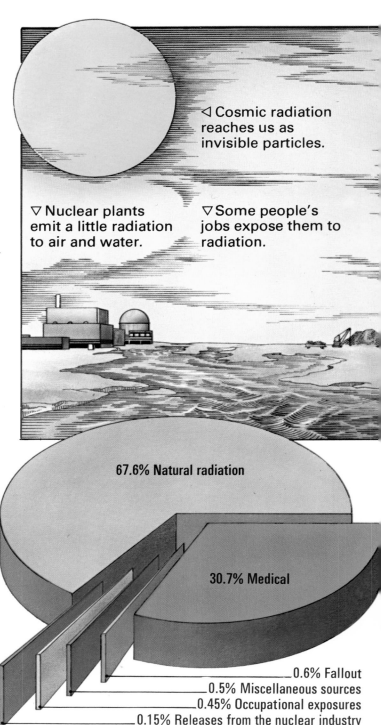

◁ Cosmic radiation reaches us as invisible particles.

▽ Nuclear plants emit a little radiation to air and water.

▽ Some people's jobs expose them to radiation.

67.6% Natural radiation

30.7% Medical

0.6% Fallout
0.5% Miscellaneous sources
0.45% Occupational exposures
0.15% Releases from the nuclear industry

Presidents Carter (USA) and Brezhnev (USSR) at the SALT (Strategic Arms Limitation Treaty) talks. Can world peace be maintained by both superpowers having a nuclear strike capability? Or does this balance of terror pose the greatest threat to peace?

△ Most radiation exposure comes from natural sources: cosmic rays, traces of uranium and thorium in the earth, and radioisotopes in our own bodies. The largest manmade sources by far are medical X-rays. The nuclear industry will normally add only a tiny trace of radiation to these other, much larger, sources.

△ Fallout from nuclear tests affects the atmosphere.

▷ Nuclear dumping has often been a source of controversy. At Windscale, in England, radioactive isotopes and plutonium traces are released by a submarine pipeline into the Irish Sea.

▷ It is claimed that the chances of a major accident occurring at a nuclear power plant are very low.

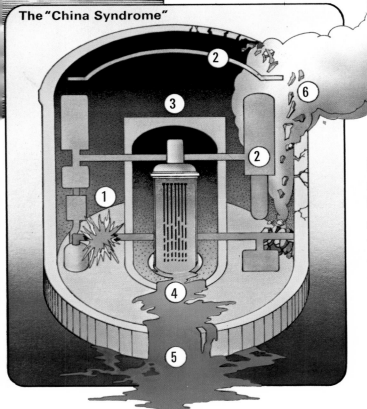

The "China Syndrome"

△ The worst accident possible – the "China Syndrome" – would occur in stages. A break on the coolant pipe (1) and failure of emergency cooling (2) causes the reactor vessel (3) to overheat, melting the fuel (4), which escapes through the concrete slab (5). The containment building (6) cracks, allowing more escapes.

If a reactor were to lose its supply of coolant, it would begin to overheat. Although the control rods could be inserted to stop the fission reaction, the radioactive decay heat given off from the fuel elements might be enough to melt them, releasing the uranium and fission products. To guard against this, reactors have emergency core-cooling systems designed to take over when their normal cooling system fails. In the Three Mile Island accident – one of the most serious yet to befall a commercial nuclear plant – the emergency system worked, but was somehow turned off by mistake. This almost caused a "fuel meltdown" – the catastrophe known as the China Syndrome.

The storage of plutonium from the spent fuel elements poses another kind of danger. Plutonium-239 can be used to make bombs. Many believe that as more nuclear plants are built around the world, the supply of Pu-239 they produce may further encourage the stockpiling of nuclear weapons, and so increase the risk of nuclear war.

31

The fast-breeder

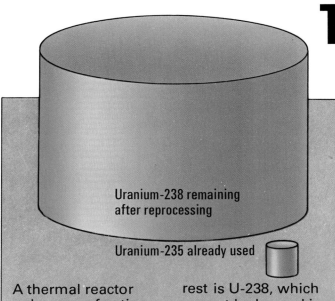

Uranium-238 remaining after reprocessing

Uranium-235 already used

A thermal reactor only uses a fraction of the uranium found in nature, the 0.7 per cent that is fissile U-235. The rest is U-238, which cannot be burned in thermal reactors. The fast-breeder reactor, however, can make use of U-238.

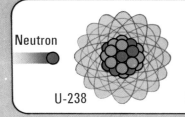

Neutron

U-238

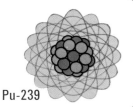

Pu-239

△ When an atom of U-238 in a reactor is hit by a neutron, it becomes an atom of a material not known in nature – plutonium-239. Pu-239, like U-235, is fissile: It can be extracted from used fuel elements and recycled.

A nuclear reactor like a PWR or an AGR (advanced gas-cooled reactor) produces plutonium in its core, as neutrons are absorbed by nuclei of uranium-238. But the amount of plutonium produced is always less than the amount of uranium burned. There is no physical reason why this should always be the case. It is quite possible to design a reactor in which more plutonium is produced than uranium burned; such a reactor is called a breeder.

A breeder needs lots of neutrons to keep it going, because so many of them are absorbed by the U-238 nuclei. To have enough left over to maintain the fission chain reaction, the designer must make sure there are plenty of neutrons to start with. We saw earlier that slow-moving neutrons are much better at causing fission than fast neutrons, which is why most reactors have moderators.

▷ Fast-breeders are cooled by liquid sodium (1), which flows upwards through the core. Sodium is a good coolant because it can carry away heat from the core more quickly than gas or water, but it needs careful handling.

Hot sodium

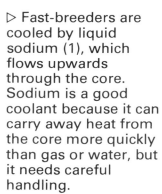

Uranium-238 blanket

Plutonium-239 core

Neutron Shield

◁ Phénix, the French prototype fast reactor at Marcoule on the Rhone, has been operating since August 1973.

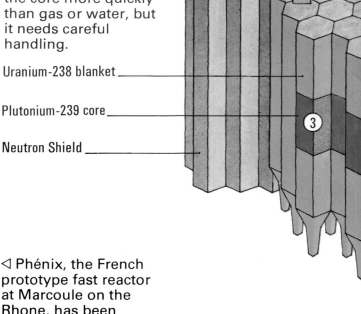

Cold sodium

The reactor cap is fitted with fueling machines for putting in new fuel elements and taking out the new Pu-239.

◁ A fast-breeder has control rods (2) but no moderator. The core of the reactor is fissile Pu-239 or U-235, or both. Around the core is a series of fuel elements, called the blanket (3), containing U-238, to be bred into Pu-239.

1 Liquid sodium
2 Control rod
3 Core of plutonium-239
4 Blanket of Uranium-238
5 Neutron shield prevents excess neutrons leaving the reactor.

The fast-breeder fuel element is divided into sections, with fissile fuel in the middle (3) and U-238 (4) towards each end. Finally, it is capped with its own neutron shield (5).

Fast neutrons do have one advantage, which is vital in breeder reactors: when they cause a fission, it tends to produce a greater number of fresh fast neutrons. The breeder-reactor designer needs every neutron he can get; so he designs his reactor around fast neutrons and calls it a fast-breeder reactor. It needs no moderator but, because fast neutrons are so inefficient at causing fission, there has to be a very high density of neutrons in a very small core. To get the heat away from such a small core needs a special coolant – liquid sodium.

Fast-breeder reactors make far better use of the world's uranium resources than other types of reactors. As well as burning the 0.7 per cent of natural uranium that is U-235, they are a fuel maker. They convert a great deal of otherwise useless U-238 into useful plutonium. By doing this they can extract from a given weight of uranium 50-60 times as much energy as can thermal reactors. The extra fuel bred by a fast-breeder reactor is recovered by reprocessing, and when enough has been accumulated it can be used to fuel a new fast-breeder. A fast-breeder of present design, however, would take about 20 years to produce enough plutonium to fuel another similar reactor.

Fusion power

Nuclear fission is not the only nuclear reaction that produces energy. There is another, even more powerful: nuclear fusion. It is nuclear fusion that provides the energy of the Sun and the stars, and nuclear fusion that produces the immense destructive power of the hydrogen bomb.

Fission is the process by which a large atomic nucleus splits to form two smaller ones. Fusion is the exact opposite, the combination of two light nuclei to form a heavier one. As it happens, the mass of the heavier element formed is slightly less than the combined masses of the two lighter ones, so just as in fission mass seems to have been lost. It has in fact been converted into energy.

The light nuclei involved in fusion are those of two isotopes of hydrogen: deuterium (which with oxygen forms heavy water, used as a moderator in some reactors) and tritium. At immensely high temperatures, these nuclei can combine to release energy. But how to achieve those temperatures and release the energy safely?

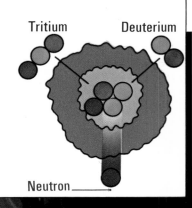

In nuclear fusion, two light isotopes, deuterium and tritium, combine to form a heavier isotope. To achieve this, they must be heated to very high temperatures and held together long enough for fusion to occur.

Tritium · Deuterium · Neutron

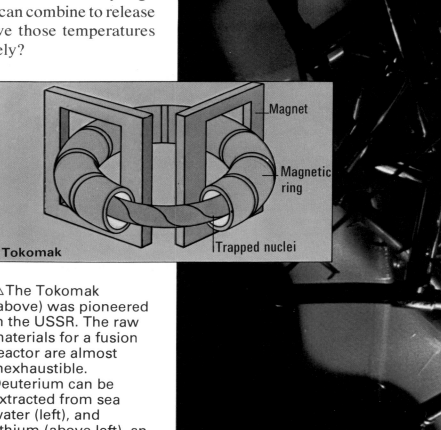

Magnet

Magnetic ring

Tokomak

Trapped nuclei

△ The Tokomak (above) was pioneered in the USSR. The raw materials for a fusion reactor are almost inexhaustible. Deuterium can be extracted from sea water (left), and lithium (above left), an element in the Earth's crust, produces tritium when bombarded with neutrons.

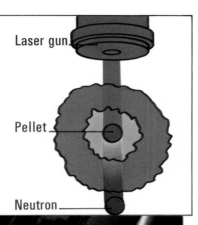

Another way of fusing light isotopes is to blast tiny pellets of deuterium and tritium with a beam of laser light. This heats and compresses them, and before the pellets can spring apart, fusion has occurred.

Laser gun

Pellet

Neutron

In the case of the hydrogen bomb, the problem is solved by using an atomic (fission) bomb to act as a trigger. But to release the power of fusion in a controlled way is very much more difficult, as scientists have discovered. One possibility would be to heat up the light atoms until they begin to fuse. But the temperatures needed would be so high that no material could withstand them. Instead, the light nuclei would have to be trapped inside "bottles" made out of magnetic fields. This might be done in a device such as the Tokomak, originally developed in the Soviet Union, in which the magnetic field forms a continuous ring – like a doughnut – so that the nuclei cannot escape. So far, no Tokomak or other fusion device has achieved the conditions necessary for fusion to take place, though physicists remain optimistic. Also, fusion using laser beams seems to work in principle.

If fusion power can be developed – and it is likely to take at least another 20 years to find out – there should be few problems with fuel supplies. Deuterium is available from water in infinite amounts, and tritium can be produced by the neutron bombardment of lithium, which is abundant.

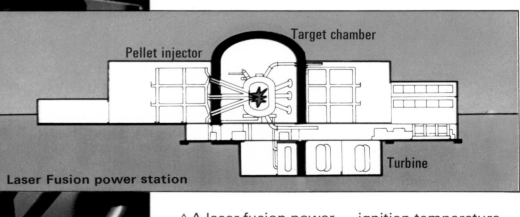

Pellet injector

Target chamber

Turbine

Laser Fusion power station

△A laser fusion power station would work in a series of explosions, each no bigger than a firecracker. Pellets of fuel would be injected one by one, at the rate of perhaps ten a second and powerful lasers would be focused on each pellet. The intense and rapid heating brings the pellet up to fusion ignition temperature (millions of degrees Celsius) before it has time to fly apart. Fusion of the light isotopes occurs, producing a tiny explosion – the output of energy – and a burst of neutrons. So far, such designs have been tested only in the laboratory, but with encouraging results.

A nuclear future?

Nuclear power has grown rapidly in the past 20 years, though not as rapidly as its supporters had hoped. Still, some expect that within the next 20 years it will be adopted as the most important source of electricity in the developed countries. Opponents of nuclear energy, in contrast, expect it to wither away and die, pointing to what they see as dwindling support for nuclear programs.

One major advantage claimed for nuclear power is that it is a proven technology that is independent of the willingness of miners to dig coal from the earth, or oil-exporting countries to continue selling oil at a reasonable price. Unlike wind, wave, solar and geothermal power, the power of the atom is considered to be reliable. It doesn't depend on the weather, and it is cheaper than energy from tidal power stations. Despite all its potential dangers, the safety record of nuclear power, as documented, is so far much better than for coal mining or oil exploration.

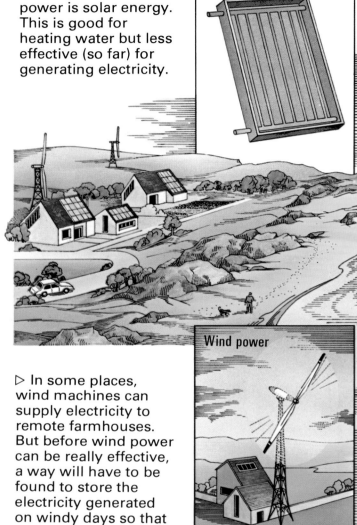

▷ One promising alternative to nuclear power is solar energy. This is good for heating water but less effective (so far) for generating electricity.

Solar power

Wind power

▷ In some places, wind machines can supply electricity to remote farmhouses. But before wind power can be really effective, a way will have to be found to store the electricity generated on windy days so that it can be used when it is calm.

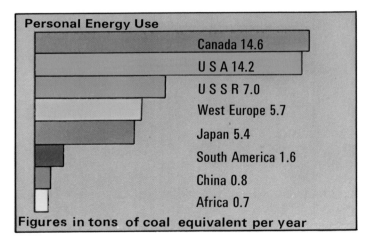

Personal Energy Use

Canada 14.6	
U S A 14.2	
U S S R 7.0	
West Europe 5.7	
Japan 5.4	
South America 1.6	
China 0.8	
Africa 0.7	

Figures in tons of coal equivalent per year

△ The amounts of energy consumed in the world vary enormously: the USA and Canada use the most. Europe and Japan are next, with the developing countries using only a fraction as much. If they are to catch up, where is all the energy to come from?

One way of easing the problem of energy is simply to use less. Large amounts can be saved by designing more efficient houses, cars that run more economically, and by reusing or recycling materials such as abandoned cars (right), instead of just throwing them away.

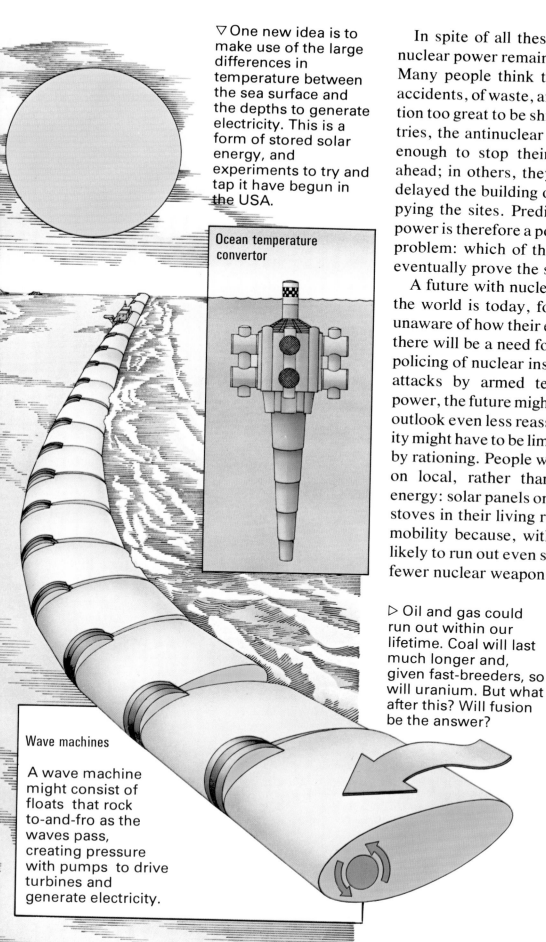

▽ One new idea is to make use of the large differences in temperature between the sea surface and the depths to generate electricity. This is a form of stored solar energy, and experiments to try and tap it have begun in the USA.

Ocean temperature convertor

In spite of all these advantages, the future of nuclear power remains clouded with uncertainty. Many people think the dangers of radiation, of accidents, of waste, and of nuclear arms proliferation too great to be shrugged aside. In some countries, the antinuclear groups have proved strong enough to stop their governments from going ahead; in others, they have disrupted plans and delayed the building of nuclear stations by occupying the sites. Predicting the future of nuclear power is therefore a political rather than technical problem: which of the two opposing forces will eventually prove the stronger?

A future with nuclear power will be much like the world is today, for most people are already unaware of how their electricity is generated. But there will be a need for tight security and careful policing of nuclear installations to guard against attacks by armed terrorists. Without nuclear power, the future might be more uncertain and the outlook even less reassuring. Supplies of electricity might have to be limited, by the high price if not by rationing. People would come to depend more on local, rather than centralized, sources of energy: solar panels on their roofs, wood-burning stoves in their living rooms. There might be less mobility because, without nuclear power, oil is likely to run out even sooner. There might also be fewer nuclear weapons. It is not an easy choice.

▷ Oil and gas could run out within our lifetime. Coal will last much longer and, given fast-breeders, so will uranium. But what after this? Will fusion be the answer?

Wave machines

A wave machine might consist of floats that rock to-and-fro as the waves pass, creating pressure with pumps to drive turbines and generate electricity.

What ☐ next?

200 years more coal

51 years more gas

28 years more oil

Index

Acknowledgements
The publishers wish to thank the following people who have helped in the preparation of this book: Central Electricity Generating Board, Commissariat à L'Energie Atomique and Electricité de France in collaboration with GAAA, Culham Laboratory (Abingdon Oxfordshire), Electricity Council (Overseas Division), Ministry of Defence, Science Research Council – The Rutherford and Appleton High Energy Laboratories (Chilton Didcot, Oxfordshire), *Daily Telegraph*, The Department of Energy.

Photographic credits
page 6, The British Petroleum Company Limited: page 7, Amax Coal Company, The British Gas Corporation: page 9, Nuclear Power Corporation: page 10, The Chessie System Railroads: page 11, The United Kingdom Atomic Energy Authority: page 12, Nuclear Power Corporation: page 13, Nuclear Power Corporation: page 16, Central Electricity Generating Board: page 18, United Kingdom Atomic Energy Authority: page 19, Zefa: page 20, M. Lambert/Gamma, Michael Abrahams: page 21, The Associated Press Ltd.: page 22, US Department of Energy: page 23, The Associated Press Ltd., Novosti Press Agency: page 24, The Radio Chemical Centre: page 25, The United Kingdom Atomic Energy Authority: page 26, Central Electricity Generating Board: page 27, Michael Abrahams, US Department of Energy: page 28, The United Kingdom Atomic Energy Authority, Nuclear Engineering Co. Inc.: page 29, Gesellschaft für Strahlen- und Umweltforschung mbH: page 30, Central Office of Information, The Associated Press Ltd.: page 31, Michael Abrahams: page 32, Commissariat à l'Energie Atomique: page 33, Commissariat à l'Energie Atomique: page 34, David Bayliss/Rida Photo Library, Oxford Scientific Films: page 35, Culham Laboratory: page 36, Jerry Mason: Endpapers, The U.K.A.E.A.